THE WAY

and

THE POWER

of

THE FORCE

THE WAY

and

THE POWER

of

THE FORCE

Based upon the Tao Te Ching
by Lao Tzu

RICHARD GANEY

IRONPRESS PUBLISHING
WINTER HAVEN, FL

The Way and the Power of The Force
Richard Ganey
Ironpress Publishing

Cataloging information
ISBN- 1-61763-010-1
ISBN- 978-1-61763-010-1

Contents

Acknowledgements

Special thanks to the following people, who took their own time to proof read and give valuable feedback. Without their help this would have take another century to complete.

Kristen Metzger
Nisha Patel
Brandon Faulkenberry
Celeste Ramirez

Foreword

This is not a book about Star Wars, or any of the wonderful science fiction world that was penned by George Lucas.

It is common knowledge that Lucas drew very heavily from the mythology teachings of Joseph Campbell, Eastern philosophy, Japanese culture, and Akira Kurosawa's cinematography. This combination was masterfully blended together to form a re-telling of a very old story; a re-telling that has become so popular that it has become part of our global culture.

It is not difficult to understand how, in today's society, the ideas, philosophy, and concepts of antiquity that Lucas drew from have become overshadowed by his creation.

In Lucas' vision, the primary religious order was a semi-monastic order he called the Jedi. They followed a belief system based on what he referred to as The Force. Interestingly there is more truth to this than most people would find comfortable to believe.

This book is a revisiting of a very ancient text. When re-imagining this text, I do make reference to Jedi, but not for the reason most people would assume.

The word Jedi can be found not only in Japanese language but also in some of the earliest writings in Egypt. In Japan, the word is Jidai. In Egypt, the word is Djedhi.

"Jedi" is a fairly common pronunciation of the Japanese word "jidai" among non-Japanese speaking people. I have personally heard many Japanese pronounce it the same. The word jidai means era or age. It is normally used to infer a period of measured time.

When talking about the Japanese and Chinese language, it is important to remember that both the written and spoken word are more abstract, more idea-based, rather than material based.

Looking at things this way and referring to someone as a Jedi, Jedi

Knight, or Jedi Master would carry the same meaning as calling them Jidai, Jidai Knight, or Jidai Master.

The usage of the pronunciation of a word is often the same as using the original word. To me, using the word spelled as "Jedi" is exactly the same as using the word "Jidai".

If we are going to call the members of philosophical order "Jedi" (Jidai) then it is not unreasonable to infer that we are talking about the period of time within which their belief system is in place.

If we look at the writings from ancient Egypt we find a tell of an order which existed there which was actually called Djedhi. The Djedhi Order of ancient Egypt would have been a point of study for Joseph Campbell and matches a lot of the aspects of the Jedi Order of George Lucas' work.

I find it extremely interesting that this order of Jedi had a symbol, called the Jed, which looks very much like a lightsaber. Most of the history of this order has been lost to antiquity, but their legend continues on.

George Lucas trademarked the word "Lightsaber". However, swords made of light, or "lightsabers" are not a new concept and have actually been around in mythology and fictional works for a long time.

Whether we are talking about flaming swords from the Bible, or magical swords of Indian kings, there are many tales of many such weapons from deep in our past. It makes one wonder what our ancestors were trying to describe as they passed on tales.

Wielders of such weapons were always referred to as having supernatural abilities, heroic status, or divine origins. They would have been hailed as bearers of the light and looked upon as guardians and keepers of the peace.

The original texts which stands as the foundation for this book have some very interesting aspects to them. Although they were initially credited as having been written around 650 BC, the texts repeatedly refer to a much earlier time. The writer of these texts is credited as being the chief librarian of the Chinese Emperor during the Zhou Dynasty and, as such, he would have had access to the whole of the Emperor's library.

As I read the texts, I can't help but feel that he was referring to much older writings and beliefs. Teachings with which he had the ability to study and which have been lost to antiquity.

In his writings, he makes constant reference to the "Way", but the "Way" of what? In most modern translations, the inference is the "The Way of Virtue", as it refers to moralistic standards. I do not believe this is the meaning of the word the writer is using. I believe he is using a much earlier meaning of the word.

Chinese characters often originate from earlier oracle script and symbols. In this case, the Chinese word "De" or "Te" evolved over time to take on a meaning of moralistic virtue. However the earlier version of "De", dating back to 1600 BC, almost a thousand years before the texts were written, implied more of a permeating energy that was present in all things and intertwined all things.

For the purpose of this book, I am referring to "Te/De" by what I believe is it's earlier meaning. Once this is done, the text take on a whole new feeling and meaning.

The Force comes alive with meaning and the text takes on a new life.

This book is not a direct translation but a re-imagining of this ancient text. This re-imagining flowed from my personal study and meditations. I am tempted as I read and re-read these writings, to think of a time when an actual order existed here on this planet.

That Order was all but destroyed in a cataclysmic event which occurred over 12,800 years ago at the time of this writing. The same order hints of its existence in almost every mythology world-wide, and whispers to us from the megalithic ruins found globally, both on dry land and below the ocean's surface.

The few members of this order which survived the event could have become the foundation for many of the world's myths and stories. This order of Jedi would have attempted to rebuild what they had known, pass on their knowledge, and try to keep the teachings of The Force alive.

Not The Force of science fiction, but The Force which flows out and permeates every particle and subparticle of the multiverse. The Force which binds us to not only to all other living creatures but to the very fabric of space and time. The Living Force whispers to us from these pages, whispers to the Self, whispers for the Jedi to re-awaken.

So if the original writings that Lao Tzu used as his foundation for his writings were much older texts, and if these texts were passed down from followers of The Force, then they would have been "Jidai" of that age. The age when people followed the ways of The Force. They would have been the first "Jedi".

Who they were and what happened to them and their order is all but forgotten.

But to me their wisdom, words, and teachings speak from the pages of Lao Tzu's work, calling for a new order of Jedi to arise.

While this seems like simple musings, I would offer up the following list of supplemental reading to tease the idea that there was a very advanced order that existed here in antiquity and that their story continues to echo through myth and legend. At the same time every year, more and more archaeological evidence is being uncovered which turns the clock back on the origins of human culture.

Magicians of the Gods - Graham Hancock
Maps of the Ancient Sea Kings - Charles H. Hapgood
Hamlet's Mill - Giorgio de Santillana
Aftershock - Brien Foerster

"We are a species with amnesia" - Graham Hancock

This codex is intended as a workbook of mindfulness and meditative reflection for the "Jedi", "Jidai", "Djedhi".

I hope that it assists in your training and helps awaken the Jedi within you.

The Codex is actually 2 books in one. The first focuses on the Way of the Force, and the second on the Power of the Force.

No further words are needed at this point. Just an open mind and the question, "What if it were all real?"

The

Way

of

The Force

Jedi Teaching 1:

Words which seek to describe The Force, no matter how eloquent, are not The Force.

To know The Force, you only need to know it.

You may walk many different paths in life, and never experience the journey. Just as you may call many things by names yet understand nothing about their essence.

Even without having been given a name, The Force formed the Universe, surrounding and binding everything.

Once it was given a name, The Force must also be said to have been the origin of all things.

If you are able to free yourself from desire, The Force will reveal its secrets to you.

If you live your life guided by desire, you will only see its illusions.

As you compare these two ideas, you will see they both flow from The Force, yet they manifest in different ways. For they together can be considered obscured and hidden in mist, because they are mysterious yet profound.

To all of the wonders of The Force, this is the way.

Jedi Teaching 2:

One can perceive what they consider as beautiful, only when it is in contrast with what they consider as ugly.

Likewise, when something is considered good, is it not only because it is in contrast to what is viewed as evil?

When someone beautiful obsesses about making themselves even more beautiful, do they not expose their ugliness?

Likewise, when a good person begins to brag or bring attention to the good things they do, do they not expose some darkness?

Thus, the Jedi should perceive all phenomena in the Universe as relative.

Being and non-being exist only relative to each other as well as the experience of whether something is difficult or easy.

To observe whether something is long or short, top or bottom, inside or outside, before or after, one must be mindful that they can only exist relative to each other.

This can also be said of speaking and listening.

Therefore, the Jedi use non-action to deal with situations.
They guide by example, not with words.

All things come and go without disrupting the Universe.

This is why the Jedi say: " It is good to create things, but do not be possessive of what you create. Do good works, without expecting anything in return. Accomplish great things, but do not seek credit or profit."

It is only when a worker approaches his work without greed, that he is sustainable.

Jedi Teaching 3:

Be mindful when praising accomplishments, as seeking adoration leads people to compete.

Do not become attached to collections of precious things, because such attachments lead people to steal.

Do not look at the things you may desire, and your heart will not be frustrated and confused by them.

Therefore, the Jedi gives the following counsel: "Breathe, clear your mind, and feel the Force around you. Release your ambitions, train in the ways of The Force, and develop strength of character."

When knowledge and desire are not what motivates you, then even the powerful cannot interfere with you.

Non-action is the way of the Force. It is to act in harmony with the Force, not striving, not forcing things.

If you can do this, then nothing is not as it should be.

Jedi Teaching 4:

Understanding the Way of the Force is likening it to an empty, bottomless bowl.

This bowl can never be filled.

The Force is ageless and because so, it is the ancestor of all things.

It smooths our roughness, and loosens our tensions and stresses.

It causes our essence to become gentler and makes us one with the Universe.

It is an invisible energy that flows through us and the entire universe, guiding us and binding us.

It precedes all.

Jedi Teaching 5:

The Force does not show preference. It treats all things equally, leaving all things to their own devices.

Likewise, Jedi should not show preference. All beings are to be treated equally, the Jedi does nothing to help nor to hinder them.

Understanding comes from imagining the Force as being like bellows.

Although it seems to be empty, it has infinite potential. With any movement, energy is moved, transformed, and released.

To write more about this would only lessen its importance.

Breathe, be mindful, and meditate on this.

Jedi Teaching 6:

Why does it seem life springs forth abundantly in the valleys, and continues to thrive from generation to generation?

This is because of the Living Force, a mysterious and profound aspect of the light side of the Force.

The Living Force is a passageway, referred to as the Root of Everything.

It is barely visible, obscured as if concealed in a haze or mist, yet we are all connected by and through it.

For those who calm themselves and listen to the Living Force, and who can decern its will, it will have unlimited uses.

Jedi Teaching 7:

The Force is perpetual and everlasting. Because the Force has no ego and does not exist for itself, it is eternal.

Because of this the Jedi do not desire to be above people, yet people admire them. Jedi do not seek to belong to any particular group, yet they are often welcome in all groups.

Is not selflessness the path to fulfillment?

This is to be meditated on.

Jedi Teaching 8:

To walk the path of the Jedi is to be like water. This is because water does not compete.

Water brings life to all living things on Earth with no expectation, yet it also submits to gravity and is drawn into the depths of the Earth. It flows not only in the beautiful mountain passes and valley streams but equally in the lowly places which people consider unappealing. In these ways water is not unlike the Force.

Consider:

When looking for a place to live, seek a good location.
When setting forth to improve your mind, seek depth.
When seeking counsel, go to a good friend.
When speaking, seek to convey the truth.
When governing, desire good judgment.
When working, be highly competent.
When choosing to act, have good timing.

To avoid the Dark Side, do not compete.

Jedi Teaching 9:

To acquire more than you need does not benefit you. Just as clinging and seeking fullfilment is not as good as knowing when to stop.

Liken this to polishing and over-sharpening a blade, for the sake of being able to cut anything. The edge will chip and the tip will break off.

The more gold and riches you acquire, the greater the likelihood that they will be stolen from you.

The self-importance that accompanies wealth and fame is often what leads to their downfall.

For the Jedi, complete your task and then let go of it. This is the way of the Force.

Jedi Teaching 10:

If you nourish your mind, body, and spirit, unifying them into one, will you ever be able to keep them from separating?

You practice the Jedi Centering Forms to become resilient and limber. But can you become like a newborn baby if you practice them hard enough?

As you meditate in the Force and see the past and future, can you ever meditate deep enough that your insights and foresights will be complete and without error?

You try to love people and bring order to the world, but do you think you can ever love hard enough to do this without knowledge and understanding?

New people are born into the world every day, but is this possible without the mother?

You can accomplish anything you put your mind to, but do you think you can do it without hard work?

This is all to say:

Nurture whatever you put forth to accomplish. Do not become attached to this goal. In your efforts and goals do not expect perfection, simply enjoy the journey. You may master your skills but results cannot be mastered.

This is another virtue of the Light Side of the Force.

Jedi Teaching 11:

All wheels have hubs. Without which the wheel would not be usable; however, it is the emptiness within the hub that make the wheel usable. It can be said that the non-being of the hub is what makes it useful.

When cups and pots are made, it is the emptiness inside that makes them usable. Here it can be said that the non-being of the cup and pot make them useful.

When houses are built, they fashion openings for doors and windows; however, it is only because of these openings that they are useful. It could be said that the house's non-being that makes it useful.

Being's purpose is to represent the potential of matter, and non-being's purpose is to make it useful.

Jedi Teaching 12:

The physical senses can be deceptive. When they become overwhelmed, they are untrustworthy.

Too many colors and lights that are too bright can hurt your eyes and make it difficult to see.

When sounds are too loud or are competing with each other, it makes them difficult to hear and understand.

Too many spices can affect the ability to taste your food.

When you are too busy chasing after things, you are unable to remain mindful and think clearly.

Things that are precious and are of great value can lead people to greed and wrongdoing.

Therefore the Jedi is to reach out and trust their feelings, not simply act on their senses. They must learn to let go of one and trust the other.

Jedi Teaching 13:

What is meant when the ancients said:

"Glory and humiliation are equally distressing."
"Regard the suffering of others as your own."

The Jedi is to consider that when fame and fortune comes to a person it can be very distressing. Equally, the loss of their fame and fortune can also be distressing. This is why the ancient teachings say, "Glory and humiliation are equally distressing."

When I personally suffer, I am driven to act quickly and decisively because it is affecting me at a personal level. But, if a situation which is sure to cause suffering does not have any contact with me, then how could it ever cause me suffering? This is why the ancient teachings say, "Regard the suffering of others as your own."

Know that when someone is able to personally convey respect to all under the sky, they can be entrusted with the world. And know also that if they are able to personally give love to all under the sky, they can be the guardian of the world.

Jedi Teaching 14:

The Force is invisible to the eyes.
The Force is inaudible to the ears.
The Force is intangible to the touch.

Considered individually, these statements may seem vague and not make sense.

Consider their meaning when put together.

The Force does not reflect light nor does it cast a shadow. The Force is always flowing, evolving, and nameless until it returns to nothingness. The Force acts as a conceptual model, having no form as if it were a shadow.

The Force is beyond explanation and imagination.

When experiencing the Force, you will not be able to fathom its beginning.

When you follow the Force, you will never lose it for it is not constrained by the bounds of time.

The Force is ancient, as are its ways. Trust in the Force and follow its ways, for even though it is ancient it still controls the present.

To seek and understand the ancient origins of the Force is the path of the Jedi.

Jedi Teaching 15:

In ancient times, before the destruction, our ancestors who were Jedi and followed the ways of the Force were amazing.

They were bringers of light; subtle, wondrous, and open. Their depths can not be fathomed because their ways are all but lost.

When attempting to describe the Masters of the Ancient Jedi Order it can be said:

They were as deliberate as when crossing thin ice.
They were as mindful as when expecting immediate danger.
They were as dignified as an honored guest.
They were as resilient as melting snow.
They were as empty as a valley.
They were as simple as an uncarved block, yet as complicated as muddy water.

Who is able to sit, breathe, and be still long enough for muddy water to settle and become clear?

Who is able to be at peace and through The Force see things?

Only those who follow the ways of the Force.

Jedi do not desire more than they need, for their trust is in the Force.

They know that they are only sustainable when they have just what they need, no more.

Jedi Teaching 16:

Relax, breathe, still yourself and clear your thoughts, empty your mind.

Reach out and feel the Force around you. Only when you are able to do this will you see that all things rise and fall. Observe their cycle.

Things come into existence, they grow and mature, multiply and develop and then they return to the Force. By returning to the Force they are once again at rest, peace, tranquil. This is the natural order of things, the cycle of the Force.

You can find our timeless nature in the cycle of The Force. To know our nature is to be enlightened, but to ignore it is disastrous. With knowledge of our timeless nature, the Jedi accepts it. With its acceptance leads the Jedi to be merciful. Being merciful is to follow the Light side of the Force and is called noble by the Jedi. To be noble is said to be like the Universe and being like the Universe is flowing in accord with the Force. In this way you are sustainable.

Death is a natural part of life, it is not extinction. It is only the end of a cycle. If you follow the ways of the Force and accept its cycles, then you can let go and the cycle is free to continue in its timeless rhythm.

Jedi Teaching 17:

A Jedi is to be knowledgeable in many things but always endeavor to not be perceived as a "know-it-all." A Jedi knows what they know and also what they do not know; never passing knowledge with no purpose.

This is seen in society, as fools go about passionately advocating some idea or belief, while other fools advocate fear and hatred of it. While all of this is going on, another group of fools mock and demean it.

Faith never aids the faithless.

Be discernful when listening to the words people speak and when watching as events unfold. What you will find is after the conversation or event has come to an end, all the fools will come forward saying "Naturally! Of course, I knew it the whole time."

Trust only in The Force, for all knowledge flows from it.

Jedi Teaching 18:

The Way of the Force is lost when one species sees itself as more important than others and when institutions of justice arise.

You will find the Darkside manifesting itself as hypocrisy wherever you find cleverness and intelligence appearing.

When family members begin to express their devotion, you know that the family affairs are not in order.

Nations are destined to fall into chaos when zealous officials hold office.

Jedi Teaching 19:

Detach yourself from holiness and deny intelligence, and people will benefit a hundred fold.

Detach yourself from selfishness and relinquish attempts to justify yourself, and maybe family affection will return.

Detach yourself from cleverness and resist greed, and people will not seek to steal from you.

As you meditate on the above statements, you may find them confusing. The truth of them can be found in this:

Seek to simplify your life.

Seek to become as unmolded clay.

Seek selflessness

Seek to tame your desires.

Jedi Teaching 20:

If you stop academics which only serve as ritual, you will stop anxiety and uncertainty. Academic formalities serve only to confuse people and are not the scholarship of the Jedi. They study The Force and all that flows from it.

Formalities as ritual are also like this.

Just consider, what difference does it make whether you answer yes or yeah?

Is it possible to measure the distance between the Lightside and the Darkside?

A person's feelings are their feelings. For those who fear, cannot not fear.

This is why it is said that fear is the path to the Darkside. Once you give into fear, left unchecked it will lead to suffering.

There are no limits to the desires and ambitions of people in the world today.

Everyone is running around craving excitement and entertainment, striving for glory and gain. They move through life as if they are at a festival or party, looking out at the world as from a high place.

But the Jedi should meditate on the following words and comtemplate their meaning:

I, alone, am indifferent, not manifesting one thought of glory or gain.
I flounder from place to place with no motive or intention.
Everyone has an overabundance of glory and advantage, yet I alone seem to have lost mine.
My mind is innocent like the innocence of a fool's mind.
Worldly people appear bright, always clarifying everything. I am very dim.
Worldly people are very sharp and clever, I am very dull.

I am aimless like the Ocean. Boundless and unattached as the wind.

Everyone else seems to be driven by desires, yet I govern my passions. I am without desire, seeking neither glory nor gain.

I am so different from others because the Force is my ally, and I value the sustenance that flows from it.

Jedi Teaching 21:

When you follow the Ways of the Force. You will grow stronger in the Force, and you will develop great character.

The Ways of the Force are so elusive, ever appearing, yet always disappearing.

We sense at the core of The Force a pattern, almost discernable, yet elusive, However, as Jedi we are sure that at its core there is a pattern, and although obscured, we know there is an essence there.

This essence is reality, because its core is Truth.

From the beginning of all things to the present time, it is the same: unnamed. But we call it the Force. It is evident in the origin of all things. How do I know of the origins of the Universe?

Because of this!

Jedi Teaching 22:

Yield and you will become whole.
Bend and you will become straight.

Empty your mind and you will become full.
Exhaust your body and you will become renewed.

Have little and you will become enriched.
Have much and you will become preoccupied.

Therefore the Jedi embraces Oneness, and thereby becomes a guide to the world.

Not looking at yourself, you become insightful.
Not talking about yourself, you make a statement.

Not advertising yourself, you will get noticed.
Not promoting yourself, you will be advanced.

The Jedi do not seek to contend, that no one in the world can contend with them.

If you doubt the truth of this teaching, then sincerely seek a state of wholeness and you will see its truth.

Jedi Teaching 23:

Have you ever wondered why gale force winds come and go, and thunderstorms normally last no longer than a day? It is because Nature expresses itself in whispers.

Even the Earth and Sky are not able to maintain such things for prolonged times. Why is it that we should expect much more from people?

Therefore, the Jedi who devoutly follows the Ways of The Force, being in alliance with The Force, creates the Way of Virtue. Together they bring both virtue and loss.

Their alliance brings virtue, as the Force brings virtue.

Their alliance brings loss, as the Force also brings loss.

Jedi Teaching 24:

You are unsteady, easily unbalanced when standing on your tiptoes, and you are quickly exhausted if you run as hard as you can.

One does not become more insightful by staring at themselves in a mirror. One does not make a worthwhile proclamation if they are talking about themselves. When one advertises themselves, they are not taken in earnest. One will not make true progress when focused on promoting themselves.

The Jedi sees these things as they would old food or like carrying excess baggage. These things lead to the Dark Side and as such are to be avoided.

Jedi Teaching 25:

There was something mysterious and incalculable that existed before the Universe came into being. It was silent, empty, singular, unique, and eternal. It flowed outward; spiraling, unfolding, and continuing without end.

You could say that this is the creator of all things: nameless. If you forced me to describe it, would it not be the way things are. If you forced me to name it, would it not still be The Force. It flows out infinitely, through everything, ebbing and flowing through all things and returning to itself.

The Force is great; the Universe is great; the Earth is great; living creatures are also great. This is because at its center there are four basic dimensions to this world, and living creatures are one of them. The Earth evolved from the Universe. The Universe evolved from The Force. The way these things evolved we call Nature.

Jedi Teaching 26:

Heaviness is the root of light, in the same way as tranquility is master of rashness.

Because of this, the Jedi travels throughout the day without losing mindfulness.

Although they travel through great cities, among the bustling streets, and in tall buildings, they trust and find peace in The Force.

How can the commander of legions be slight? It is not possible.

Light standards lose the root and rash standards lose control.

Jedi Teaching 27:

The finest travel does not leave traces of its passing.
The finest words flow and are not stuttered.
The finest calculations do not have to be worked out on paper.
The finest door lock has no locking mechanism yet it cannot be unlocked.
The finest binding is not bound with the tangible, yet it cannot be untied.
This is the splendor of conservation of energy, conservation of movement.

The Jedi's nature is to be the best at restoring people, viewing no one as unimportant or disposable. Likewise, to be the best at restoring things, viewing nothing as useless and disposable. This is because the Jedi is to act from insight of what is hidden inward not what is seen outward.

Thus the best of people serve as examples for the people who are not so good, and the people who are not so good serve as potential to become the best of people. For if one fails to value the example and refuses to love the potential - although they may be clever - they are greatly confused.

To understand the secret wonders of the Force, one must understand this, for this is the essence of those secrets.

Jedi Teaching 28:

Know the masculine but keep to the feminine, and you will be as a little valley to the world. Like that little valley, the eternal nature of virtue will not leave you. Thereby, returning you to your original state of when you were born.

Know glory but maintain humility, and you will be as a big valley to the world. Like that big valley, the eternal nature of virtue cannot be corrupted in you, thereby, returning you to your original state as an uncarved block.

Know the Dark Side but keep to the Light Side, and you will be as the world's guide. As a guide, the eternal nature of virtue will not waiver in you, thereby, returning you to your original state, not being polarized by the duality.

Once the uncarved block is cut, it makes pawns. The Jedi's use of the block makes leaders. Thus, great sculpting does not mean it has to be cut down in size!

Jedi Teaching 29:

Jedi know that those who would seek to force their will upon the world, with what they think will improve it, will not succeed.

Planets are spiritual vessels. You cannot force them to bend to your will, nor can you control or possess them for your own profit. When anyone tries to force their will and control any world, they will ruin it. When they try to possess it, they will lose it.

It is important to be mindful that sometimes things lead, and sometimes they follow. Sometimes things are hard, and sometimes they are soft. Sometimes breath in, and sometimes breath out. Sometimes things go fast, and sometimes things go slow. Sometimes things grow powerful, and sometimes they grow weaker. Sometimes they rise, and sometimes they fall.

This is why the Jedi renounce excesses, renounce extravagance, and renounce extremes. For them they trust that The Force will bring to them all they need and in the time and manner in which they need it.

Jedi Teaching 30:

It is in understanding the ways of The Force that one learns how to be a good leader, not by threatening people with their weapons. Such actions invite revenge.

There is a saying of ancient times that where a great army camps that bushes of thorns rise up, and where great wars are fought that the land is left barren and devastated.

When settling matters of contention, seek a good outcome and;
If force must be used, know when to stop. Do not be excessive.
It is important that once an acceptable outcome is reached, be mindful and do not give in to pride or arrogance. Do not act self-righteously and do not allow greed to enter into the resolution.

There is nothing wrong with seeking a good outcome to a matter of contention, but not by dominating others.

When people follow and respect the magnificently strong, you know it is not of the Lightside of the Force. And, anything of the Darkside is not sustainable and will soon end.

Jedi Teaching 31:

Weapons of war and weapons whose sole purpose is to be used to kill are a shameful thing; all living things hate them. Those who follow the Ways of the Force, want nothing to do with weapons designed for killing.

Jedi abandon all weapons save their saber. Which they use for training and defense, never for attack. They understand violence is sometimes necessary, but they find no joy in it or in death.

Because weapons used for killing are shameful things, they are not the tools of the Jedi and the followers of The Force. Peace and quiet are most precious to us.

A military victory is never a cause to celebrate. Those who celebrate victory and the killing of their enemy take pleasure in the slaughter and have embraced the Darkside. If someone takes pleasure in the slaughter, forever will the Darkside dominate their destiny. The slaughtered will forever haunt them; their life will be without joy and they will not bear fruit.

Jedi Teaching 32:

The eternal nature of The Force is to be nameless, formless. Appearing unassuming and powerless, yet in all the world nothing can overpower it.

If the world's leaders were able to cultivate it, all things would find their place and yield. The Universe and the world would be in harmony, and their sweet intoxicating rain would fall. People would know peace and order, there would be no need for laws, rules, and regulations.

All the troubles in the world began when we started naming everything. As a species, we have fallen into the trap of believing that if we simply know the name of something, somehow, that imparts understanding of its essence to us. We have now come to the trouble of having too many names, labels, and categories for things. You would have thought that people would have learned when to stop.

The Jedi is to be particularly mindful of this problem, they avoid confusion by not mistaking "form" or a name for the essence of a thing.

To give an example, The Force flows throughout the Universe. Like water through a valley, It flows from Its source to a brook,then to a river, and then the sea. Knowing this do any of these names actually describe the essence of water?

Jedi Teaching 33:

One may become clever learning about another. However, true insight comes from learning about yourself.

You may become powerful if you conquer someone else. However. You will surely become empowered if you conquer yourself.

Living in moderation and knowing when you have enough can make you rich. However, practicing empowerment will imbue you with willpower.

It is often said that someone endures if they demonstrate longevity in tasks they set themselves to. It is also said of those who have attained some position or title.

But to truly be enduring it is important - that even though the individual may die - the ideas and principles they value, do not.

Jedi Teaching 34:

The Force surrounds and connects everything in the Universe, flowing through all living things, manifesting itself in both the Lightside and the Darkside.

All living things depend on it, none are excluded, regardless of whether they can feel it or not.

It is used for accomplishments, yet it takes no credit for them. It also nourishes and cares for all living things, yet it does not seek to control them.

The Force desires nothing, and because of this, you could call it a small thing. However, all living things must return to it in the end, yet it does not impose its will on them. Because of this, you could say that The Force is great.

In the virtue of The Force not making itself great, it actually enables itself to be great.

Jedi Teaching 35:

When you follow The Force, the Universe will yield to you.

No harm will come to followers of The Force, only peace and order. They are free to enjoy each moment as a guest enjoys music and food.

However, those who simply sit and talk about The Force, seem empty and hollow. Their words are bland and tasteless.

The true reach of The Force is unseen. Its wisdom is unheard, but its power and usefulness is unlimited.

Jedi Teaching 36:

The Jedi must always remain mindful of the contrasting nature of the Universe and the way The Force manifests itself.

When we see something weakened, we must remember that it had to first have been strong.

When we see something shrinking, it must have first been larger and spread out.

When we see something knocked down, it must have first been raised up.

One of the wonderful secrets of the Lightside of The Force is that the soft and flexible shall overcome the hard and strong. The strongest and mightiest fish are bound to the soft and yielding depths of the Ocean, just as mortal weapons will never defeat the human spirit.

Jedi Teaching 37:

No matter what name people call The Force by, nor if it is not named at all, it leaves nothing not done.

If the leaders of the modern world would follow the ways of The Force, everything would change of its own accord. The change would be so complete that when desire manifests, because of the oneness the world would have in The Force, it would be easily restrained.

Eventually, people would be able to govern their passions and desires to the extent that desire would lose its power. In the heart where desires and passions have no power, there is tranquility.

The planet would find peace of its own accord.

The

Power

of

The Force

Jedi Teaching 1:

The greatest virtue is virtue that comes without effort, virtue that is not attempting to be virtuous. The worst type of virtue is virtue that is superficial, forced, or 'put on'.

The greatest virtue acts in accord with The Force. It simply exists with no outside effort or interference. Even though the greatest of human concepts appear to be effortless, they are still not in accord with The Force and require outside effort.

The greatest form of justice requires great outside effort and action. Even the best rules and regulations require effort, and we find when that fails people use violence to attempt to enforce the rules.

The ancient Jedi had a saying: "When people stop following the Ways of The Force, the concept of virtue appears. When people lose virtue, humanistic concepts and systems of justice appear. When justice is lost, many rules are written." Rules being subjective and drawing dependence on the truths as seen by the writer begin the decent into chaos and the Darkside.

The ability to see the future is an ability which flows from The Force for those who follow its Ways. However, without knowledge and guidance from The Force it is the beginning of foolishness.

This is why the Jedi focus on what lays beneath the surface of things, and ignore the superficial. They concentrate on the fruit and not the flower. They reject the one and receive the other.

Jedi Teaching 2:

In ancient times, before the cataclysm, this world was one with The Force.

In this oneness, the sky was clear, and the Earth sang with resonance.

The oneness brought strength to the spirits of Jedi and non-Jedi alike, and valleys flowed with abundance. All living things lived in harmony in the oneness of The Force.

The Jedi of the ancient order were one with The Force. They taught and guided the leaders of the many costal cities in the Ways of The Force. Their actions were upright, they maintained the peace, yet they did not interfere.

Since the events which destroyed the Jedi, destroyed the cities of the world, and brought the Earth out of harmony with The Force, the ways of the Jedi have been forgotten and the ingenuity of men has taken its place.

The sky is no longer clear, but polluted.

The Earth no longer sings with resonance, but is threatened with pollution and erosion.

The strength which used to flow from The Force, is now threatened by exhaustion.

The life and abundance of the valleys, is in danger of withering.

The living things of the Earth, living out of the oneness, are threatened with extinction.

The leaders of the world, without the guidance of the Jedi, have turned to the Darkside and brought the world to the edge of ruin.

Humility is the foundation of honor, just as low is the foundation of high. You will often hear the leaders of the world and people of high status say it is lonely at the top, that their actions are unappreciated, and that they are unable to accomplish things because of one reason or another. Are they not attempting to rely on the perception of humility to operate?

So the highest renown of the world is not renown at all. Do not desire to be like shiny gems, instead as a lowly stone which has sunk deep into the ground.

Jedi Teaching 3:

The ebb and flow of The Force can be seen in the cycles of the Universe and in nature.

Only by letting go, yielding, and not striving can The Force be used.

All of the Universe is the manifestation of being, yet where did being originate? Being originated from non-being.

Jedi Teaching 4:

There are three types of students who begin the journey toward becoming a Jedi:

The superior student; As they learn the Ways of The Force, they diligently practice all they learn.

The mediocre student; As they learn the Ways of The Force, they periodically practice what they learn. Sometimes they remember, sometimes they forget.

The inferior student; As they learn the Ways of The Force, they laugh loud and uncontrollably. You see if they did not laugh, it would not truly be The Force.

The light of the Ways of The Force, sometimes seem like darkness. Growing in strength and moving forward with The Force, sometimes feels like you are moving backwards. Walking the path of the Jedi, sometimes feels like you are bound up with rope.

You can liken great virtue to a valley, and great purity as soil.

Does it not feel like when someone is too virtuous that they are often lacking?

Do you not hear and feel the contrivance of orthodox institutions when they speak of virtue?

Through this, their true being seems concealed.

The ancient Jedi Masters would say: "The greatest frames are the ones without joints; the greatest talents take the most time to accomplish; the greatest sounds are the hardest to hear; the greatest forms take no shape".

The true Way of The Force is concealed within, unnamed. In this way, The Force nourishes and fulfills all.

Jedi Teaching 5:

Through The Force can be found the Oneness of the Universe. Yet, in this oneness can also be perceived the duality of the Lightside and the Darkside. Thru the Oneness and the Duality of The Force, we see it brought all things into being.

Through all things, The Force flows, both the Lightside and the Darkside. Yet because of the interaction, between the Lightside and Darkside, through all living things the Living-Force flows. Its purpose is to balance the Light and the Dark, to create life-giving energy. For those who feel it, it provides knowledge and gives strength, health, and new life.

The Ways of the Force are beyond understanding. Yet, the Oneness and the Duality can be seen all around us, constantly balancing itself. Why do you think it is that some benefit from their loss, or they lose because of their benefits? It is because of how the Duality and the Oneness relate.

The teachings here are the same as in many teachings. Anger and aggression are not sustainable, people who live their life following this path do not meet their ends with peace.

This is so simple, yet so few people follow it.

Jedi Teaching 6:

The greatest flexibility overcomes the greatest firmness. Non-being penetrates places that have no opening. This is how to know that non-contrivance has benefit.

No words can teach it, only non-contrivance can reveal its benefits. This explains why so few understand it.

Jedi Teaching 7:

Which do you value more? Your good reputation or your health?
Which do you price more? Your health or your possessions?
Which will harm you the most? Gain or loss?

Attachment has with it a great cost, and clinging to possessions will surely lead to loss.

The Jedi is to know when they have enough, and therefore do not falter.

The Jedi is to know when to stop, and therefore avoid danger.

To know and apply these things allow anyone, not just Jedi, to live a sustainable life.

Jedi Teaching 8:

Consider that great accomplishments always seem unfinished, as they are constantly being used and therefore are never done.

Consider that great plentitude seems empty, but it usefulness is inexhaustible.

Consider these things:

The longest and straightest of lines appear to bend.
The greatest of craftsmen appear to be very simple.
The greatest of eloquence seems inarticulate.

Activity overcomes the cold.
Stillness overcomes the heat.

Calm and clarity are the standard for the Jedi.

Jedi Teaching 9:

There was a time when the people of this planet followed the Ways of The Force, there was order and peace, stray horses and wild animals did not wander onto plowed fields.

Now the people do not follow the Ways of The Force and chaos abounds.

Armies and the machines of war trample the fields which have withered up and been over grown with weeds.

The greatest of sins is ungoverned desire.

The greatest misfortune is not knowing when enough is enough.

The greatest fault is greed.

Thus knowing when enough is enough is the gateway to being content with what you have.

Jedi Teaching 10:

You do not have to walk out of your door, to know all that is in the Universe.

You do not have to look out the window to see the Ways of The Force.

The truth be known the more time you spend searching, the less you actually know.

This is why the Jedi does not move but knows. They do not see but know what it is. They do not strive, yet they accomplish.

Their knowledge and understanding comes from The Force.

Jedi Teaching 11:

If you work passionately at becoming knowledgeable, you will find that every day you become a little more knowledgeable.

If you work passionately at becoming wealthy, you will find that every day you acquire a little more wealth.

If you work passionately at learning the Ways of The Force, you will find that every day something is stripped away from you.

You will find the Way strips away more and more, until it teaches you how not to impose your timing on things. After time, you will see that when you do not impose your timing on things and when you do not strive, that nothing is left undone.

People of today believe the secret to success, and achieving all their dreams, is to be enterprising; however, those who are enterprising and have achieved success and fulfilled their dreams, often find it is never enough.

Jedi Teaching 12:

The Jedi does not have biases favoring one point of view over another. They focus on the needs of the people and on what The Force has revealed to them.

They are kind to those who are kind to them, and yet they are also kind to those who are not kind to them. In this way, they embody the essence of kindness.

They trust those who they know can be trusted, yet they also place trust in those who have been show not to always be trustworthy. In this way they embody the essence of trust.

Jedi are mindful that their thoughts remain focused on the moment, whether they are in the temple or out in the universe. Those not of The Force often perceive the Jedi as preoccupied, or muddled in their behaviors and are often confused at the humble and reserved way they act when around others.

People pay attention to the Jedi, watching them and listening to their words. The Jedi know that all life is from The Force.

Jedi Teaching 13:

There is an old saying that when a person is confronted with a life or death incident, that three out of ten will live, three out of ten will die. It is also said that for those who appear at death's door, three out of ten will survive and continue to live. This is not difficult to understand if you know that The Force flows through all of us, and the level of connection with The Force varies from person to person.

Those who are strong with The Force travel out in all manner of places never striving with the buffalo or tiger. In battles, no weapons can pierce their armor. Because the buffalo's horns can find no place to gore, the claws of the tiger no flesh to rip, and weapons can find no weakness in the armor to pierce.

This is because for those who are one with The Force, there is no place for death to enter in.

Jedi Teaching 14:

The Force gives life, the power of The Force nurtures it. The environment shapes it, and love makes it whole.

Thus all living creatures respect The Force and honor its power.

When The Force is respected and its power is honored, all things resolve themselves without intervention.

Thus, The Force gives life and the power of The Force feeds it, develops it, cares for it, shelters it, comforts it, nurtures it, and protects it.

The Force may give life, but it does not act possessively of it. The Force provides but it does not seek to dominate. The Force sows seeds and tends to them but does not harvest them.

This is a principle essence of The Force.

Jedi Teaching 15:

If we consider that The Force manifest the Universe, then we can use the analogy that The Force is like the Mother of Creation.

When we recognize the Mother, then we immediately recognize who the children are. Once we realize we are those children, we know we should obey the Mother.

Once we know this, there is no more fear of death. We can bury our bodies and know there is no danger awaiting us. For what mother would harm their child when they return?

Be one with The Force. Close your mouth, calm yourself, and when death comes, you will meet it without a struggle. Or, you can close yourself off from The Force, scurry around acting busy, chatter and talk, but when death comes, you will face it with no resolve in your heart.

See the small and gain insight, obey the soft and become strong, use your intelligence but never forget your insight.

It has always been true that clinging to life and not being able to accept death brings disaster and suffering.

Jedi Teaching 16:

Anyone having good sense would follow the teachings of the Ancient Jedi. They knew to follow the Lightside of The Force and constantly cautioned of the dangers of the Darkside.

The Way of the Jedi, to follow the Lightside of The Force, is not difficult to follow. Its way is clear and easy to walk for those who stick to the path. But people are inherently fond of short-cuts and trying to find an easier way. The path to the Darkside is littered with what appear to be short-cuts and easier paths to become one with The Force.

They live their lives in fear:

Fear of not having a home as beautiful as those around them. They have beautifully decorated homes, yet their fields are not properly tended and overgrown with weeds.

Fear of not being adorned as finely as those around them. They dress beautifully and adorn themselves with the finest jewelry, yet they have not saved for tomorrow.

Fear of not being able to defend themselves and of being perceived as weak.

They carry deadly weapons around and seek contention.

Fear of not being accepted by the people around them. They eat and drink to excess, acquiring more wealth than they need. They have forgotten the greater the wealth, the greater chance that someone will rob them. Having this excess tempts people to steal from them.

Fear leads to anger, anger to hatred, and hatred ultimately causes suffering.

Jedi Teaching 17:

When the roots of a plant or tree run deep, it cannot easily be uprooted. When something is held with a firm grip, it is not easily lost. Children should honor and keep alive the values and teachings of their ancestors.

When you nurture a person, your values become real for them and you. When you nurture your family, your values surround them and you. When you nurture your community, your values are shared and passed on through the generations. Nurture your nation and your values will be spread by the people. Nurture the entire planet and universe and your values become immortal.

So, in judging your values, judge your person as a person, your family as a family, your community as a community, your nation as a nation, your planet as a planet, and the universe as the universe.

How do I know of the Universe? This is it!

Jedi Teaching 18:

When considering your connection to The Force, compare it to that of a newborn child.

It is known that neither the snake nor the scorpion will attack a newborn. It is also very rare that a tiger maul it nor a hawk try to grab it.

The newborn's bones are soft and pliable, but its grip is very strong.

It has no use for its sexual organs, yet they are fully formed. This is the essence of The Force.

It is able to cry all day without getting tired and straining its voice. This is the harmony of The Force.

Knowing the harmony of The Force is enlightenment.

So consider and weigh your connection to The Force using this example.

Seeking excitement and adventure are often found from pushing the limits of life.

You may find you can control great power if you channel The Force through you.

These things rise and fall, reach a peak and then decay. They are reckless.

This reckless behavior is not the Way of The Force, and whatever does not follow the Ways of The Force comes to an early end.

Jedi Teaching 19:

People who have wisdom and are knowledgeable about a subject do not feel the need to force their opinion and experience on others. Those who are not wise and have limited knowledge about a subject always feel the need to force their opinion on others and to embellish their understanding of the topic.

Be calm, quiet, and guard closely the words that you speak.

Be at peace, still, and be mindful of those you surround yourself with.

Blunt the sharpness of your tongue and actions.

Let go of those things which you are attached to.

Dim your brilliance.

Become one with The Force, for this is from where knowledge and strength flow.

Someone who is one with The Force will find they no longer chase after things, yet they also do not attempt to avoid them. They help no one but also harm no one. They do not seem to progress, but they also do not fall behind. Even though this behavior may be very confusing, it is the way The Force behaves.

Jedi Teaching 20:

When there is order within a country, it is at peace and runs in harmony. When there is disorder within a country, it wages war and struggles. Peace in the world can never be achieved through strife and struggling.

To know this is true; you must simply look around you.

Is it not true that where there are rules and regulations, the people are poorer and go without?

Is it not true that where people have more and more weapons, the nation is more dangerous?

Is it not true that the more technologically advanced we become, life becomes faster and more stressful?

Is it not true that the more things we make against the law, the more people become criminals?

This is why the Jedi say:

I practice non-action and the people thrive on their own.
I love peace and the people maintain order on their own.
I never strive and the people prosper by their own hand.
I have no desires and the people live a simpler life.

Jedi Teaching 21:

It is often the case that when governments have few regulations and do not meddle in the affairs of their people, that the people are simple. Likewise, when governments are oppressive and meddle in the affairs of their people, that the people are forced to become clever.

Understand that good fortune comes from bad events, and bad fortune often hides beneath good events. The outcome of these are difficult to see because the future is always in motion.

People are often confused when the people they hold in high regard break the laws of the land, and when good people act badly. This originates from a perspective of duality, and those seeing only the duality, do not see the Force.

This is why the Jedi trims without cutting,
They Point without piercing.
They are straightforward, but not to an extreme.
They bring the light, but are not blinding.

Jedi Teaching 22:

The best manner to care for people and to be in harmony with nature is to practice ecology.

Ecology is the art of learning the nature of how things grow and develop. In the process of learning the nature of how things grow and develop, one will acquire virtue. With this virtue, one will understand there is nothing which cannot be overcome and there is no limit to what you can do.

A great country could be built upon the foundation of these virtues, a country which would have sustainability to the living creatures. This country would have the knowledge required to look ahead and plan for the future of its people.

Jedi Teaching 23:

Rulers of a great country should govern in the same manner you would cook a small fish.

If the Ways of The Force are manifested throughout the Universe, then the Darkside will have no power.

This should not be misunderstood. The Darkside would have power, but it would not harm the people.

Not only would the Darkside not harm the people, but the Lightside also would not harm them either. Through this balance and harmony, peace is manifest and virtue would flow throughout the Universe.

Jedi Teaching 24:

A truly great country protects, nurtures, and helps facilitate the social interactions of its people. It could be said that great countries are like the mothers of the world.

The feminine overcomes the masculine through acceptance. This acceptance acts like it is subordinate, in that it nurtures.

So if a great country wants to win the loyalty of a smaller country, then it attends to the needs of the smaller country, thereby winning the smaller country. Likewise, if a smaller country wishes to align itself with the great country, then they should attend to the needs of the great country, thereby winning alliance with the great country.

So you can see that by attending to the needs of the other, one wins and one is won.

A great country's wish should be for it to have good people as its citizens, and a smaller country simply wants stability and jobs for its citizens. So for both countries to get what they want, they should both attend to the needs of each other.

Jedi Teaching 25:

The Force flows through and binds the entire Universe. It flows and nurtures not just those who follow the Lightside but also those who follow the Darkside.

We honor those who speak eloquently, those who accomplish noble deeds, and those who follow the Lightside. But should we abandon and hold in disregard those who have done none of these?

No greater gift can be given to someone than to teach them of The Force and to show them how to follow its Way.

An ancient saying of the Jedi Masters was; "Seek and you will find, ask and you will receive, knock and it will be opened." Do not all people when having committed a transgression, seek forgiveness? This is why grace, mercy, and forgiveness are the among the highest of virtues, to Jedi and non-Jedi alike.

Jedi Teaching 26:

The secret in following the way of the Jedi is to act without acting, strive without striving, and to sense without using your senses. At first this will seem contradictory and confusing, but one who would follow The Force and be a Jedi, should meditate on this.

All things which are great did not start that way; they all started as something smaller. A vast quantity of anything did not start that way; it always started as few. All hardship appears unrewarding yet rewards with wisdom and patience.

The Jedi are mindful of the simplicity in things others consider complex, and know that to achieve greatness in anything comes from many small deeds. Thereby the Jedi know that in seeing the simple in the complex is the key to making difficult tasks simple.

This is why the Jedi strive not to act great, thereby accomplishes great things.

Do not be too quick to make promises as they do not instill a sense of trust in people. Do not rush things, even things which seem simple and insignificant, because in doing so you cause mistakes to be made and many difficulties arise.

This is why the Jedi boldly confronts many small things and find none of them difficult to accomplish.

Jedi Teaching 27:

When one is in harmony with The Force, it is easy be at peace and to avoid all manner of trouble. But when one falls out of harmony with The Force, becoming rigid and brittle, they are easily shattered, and their life is easily drawn into contention.

Be mindful and trust in The Force. When one with The Force, trust your feelings to know when to act prior to being required to act. Know that the time to restore order is prior to confusion and chaos taking hold.

The essence of this can be found all around us. The mightiest of trees began as mere seeds. The tallest of buildings began as mere dirt. And a journey of a thousand miles begins with a mere step.

When you attempt to force the timing of something, it often leads to failure.

When you cling to something and are attached to it, it often leads to losing it.

The Jedi do not force the timing of things and therefore do not fail. They are mindful not to desire and cling to things and therefore they do not lose.

People often become restless as they approach the completion of something, they either rush to finish or lose focus on their task. This impatience often leads to failure. One should maintain consistency throughout any task, finishing the task as they began it, thereby their task will not fail.

The Jedi desire to not be trapped by having desires. They do not value and seek possessions and valuable items. They are knowledgeable, yet do not flaunt their knowledge or mastery. Thereby avoiding the losses that others have.

The Way of the Force helps everything in the Universe exist according to its nature, not forcing against its nature.

Jedi Teaching 28:

The Jedi of the ancient order understood the responsibilities that come with the powers that The Force bestows. They understood the price associated with misusing these powers.

In their dealings with both other Jedi and non-Jedi, they promoted keeping one's thoughts and way of life simple. For they understood the difficulties that enter into people's lives when they act clever.

This is why they refrain from trusting politicans because their cleverness makes them untrustworthy, and they run the nation to the edge of ruin. However, when you find simple government officials who do away with cleverness, that nation prospers and grows.

It should be understood, that both positions flow as a pattern from The Force. Understanding how this is so is a fundamental virtue all Jedi must have. This fundamental virtue reaches deep and wide. It is what causes all things to return to their nature, return to The Force.

Jedi Teaching 29:

There is a saying that all rivers flow to the Sea. If you consider this, the Sea then brings life and governs hundreds of valleys. It is because of the Sea being beneath them, that allows the Sea to rule to the hundreds of valleys.

When people seek to be in charge of something and to lead people, they should speak with humility and respect.

When the Jedi take leadership of something, they are able to lead without oppressing those they lead. They lead by example and show the way, but do not stand in the way of the people who follow them. Therefore they are welcome throughout the universe and people do not tire of their company.

This is because they refrain from competing, and in not competing, nothing can compete with them.

Jedi Teaching 30:

The whole universe recognizes that the Way of the Force is great and that it is unique. It's uniqueness is why it endures, or else it would have been forgotten like all the other ancient ways.

Even though it is great and unique, it is really quite simple. The Jedi have three pillars and three core values which all Jedi understand, possess, and maintain.

All Jedi hold and maintain three pillars as valuable to themselves and to the Order. The first is developing and cultivating their connection to The Force. Second is knowledge,of the Ways of The Force, which comes from experiencing. The third is self-discipline, which comes from constant training.

Coupled with this are the three core values which all Jedi possess and maintain. The first of these, above all else, is love. The second is ecology. The third is not trying to be superior to those around you.

Through love come many courageous acts.

By being ecological you are able to extend generosity.

By not trying to be superior to those around you and maintaining humility, you will cause many people to follow your example.

In the world today there is a dead-end street that many people are on. They turn away and reject love, yet they seek courage.

They reject ecology and economical thinking, yet they want generosity.

They treat others with pride and arrogance, reject humility, yet desire to lead people and have people follow them.

They are blind to the fact that it is because of love, that their offense wins battles, and their defenses hold.

Can it not be seen that even though The Force and the Universe nourish us, that it is love that protects us?

Jedi Teaching 31:

Powerful Jedi always remember:

To always be mindful of your feelings, never strike out in anger and aggression.

When forced into a contest of arms, never allow anger to guide you.

Do not let pride and arrogance enter into a contest, as this often leads to grudges.

When leading, ground yourself in humility and do not place your worth above those you lead.

This is the teaching of non-striving. From this teaching, you can learn how to manage power and responsibility. From this teaching, you will learn how to become one with The Force.

Jedi Teaching 32:

In antiquity, there was an idea among the leaders of militaries. "I refuse to be the aggressor in a conflict. My actions will always be in defense. I would rather yield a foot than to take an inch."

This is teaching how to defend oneself and how not to become the aggressor. This is teaching how to deal with contention without being contentious. It is teaching how to be mindful of your surroundings not looking for a fight, but at the same time prepared to defend.

In conflicts, do not make the mistake of disrespecting your opponent. In disrespecting your opponent, you not only stray from the teachings of the Jedi, but you also may fuel your opponents resolve.

Also remember that you should never take joy in the defeat of an enemy, for after a battle there is always a time of regret felt by the victor.

Jedi Teaching 33:

The teachings of the Jedi are easily understood, and following the Ways of The Force are easily practiced. Yet in all the Earth, few seek to understand the teachings, and no one practices the Way of The Force.

It is so easy to discern that the teachings of the Jedi originate from an ancient source, that the Ways of The Force have an ancient precedent. Yet people ignore the ancient teachings, ignore the Way of The Force, and refuse to acknowledge the ancient Jedi order.

It is true there are some that still feel The Force. Those who understand the ancient teachings are very few. Those who study and practice the Ways of The Force are special.

They are special because they will ensure the continuance of the Jedi. And even though they may dress plain, with humility, their heart is of precious gems.

Jedi Teaching 34:

It is always best to know when you do not know something. To not know how to recognize and admit when you do not know something is like having a sickness.

Whoever is tired of being sick, of being incapable of doing anything but be sick, will rise up and find a way to shed that sickness.

Jedi have shed that sickness. They are tired of the sickness and they have cast it off like skin they have outgrown.

Jedi Teaching 35:

If people disregard the possibility of bad things happening and do nothing to prevent them, then it is only a matter of time before those things happen.

In your travels, be unbiased about the way people live.

Be respectful of their home, whether it is shabby and broken down, or if it is a mansion.

Be un-biased about the manner in which people earn a living. Whether their handy work is crude and rough, or refined and beautiful. Look at each on its own merit.

Be mindful of the demands you place on people who you hire to do work for you. If your demands are not oppressive then the workers will not resist and revolt against their tasks.

This is why the Jedi meditates on self-discovery and the insight that this brings.

They do not display their skills for show or to demean another. The Jedi respects the Ways of The Force and they train with focus and seriousness of purpose; however, they are also mindful not to take themselves too seriously or overestimate their value and skills.

Therefore, they reject arrogance and choose humility.

Jedi Teaching 36:

Courageous and daring people will face a fight to the death with no reservation, but people who have no courage and take no chances will seek a safe place to cower in.

Only societies seem to place merit in one over the other, and call one of them good and the other bad. But from all appearances, The Force is unbiased and does not favor either. The reason for this is unclear and seemingly beyond our comprehension.

This is a topic of much meditation for the Jedi.

The Force does not appear to struggle, yet its outcome is good. It does not directly speak, yet it makes good responses. It asks for nothing, yet has whatever is needed. It is serenely calm, yet is prepared for all.

The reach of The Force is vast, flowing through all things, binding the Universe together, yet nothing is ever lost.

Jedi Teaching 37:

When a person has lost all respect for death, it is of no avail to threaten them with death.

It is the nature of humanity that they fear death. Why is it then, that people still continue to commit capital crimes even though the government arrests and executes them?

In the order of the Universe, there is a master executioner who's very nature is the taking of life.

Anyone who attempts to assume the role of this master executioner is like a novice woodworker trying to match the skills of a master woodworker. He is destined to cause serious injury to himself.

Jedi Teaching 38:

Why are people in the world starving? Because of the greed of men. Governments enact unreasonable taxes and those in power demand unreasonable percentages. Greed is the reason there is starvation across the world.

When you find people rebelling and being difficult to govern, it is because the government and leaders make too many rules and regulations. This is the reason people become difficult to govern.

Likewise, when you see people thrill-seeking and taking death too lightly, it is because they seek things which give them the sensation of living. It is because they have lost touch with the essence of living which has caused them to take death too lightly.

Those who value the essence of living, do not force life to happen, but welcome life with serenity and understanding.

Jedi Teaching 39:

Living people are pliable and soft, yet in death they become rigid and hard.

As with all living things on Earth, animal and plant, they are flexible and soft. However, in death they wither and become hard and inflexible.

It can be said that things that are rigid and hard are disciples of death, and things that are flexible and soft are disciples of life.

This is why an Army that is hard and rigid is easily defeated, and a tree that has become hard and rigid is easy to fell.

Relative to each other, the hard and inflexible is inferior, and the soft and flexible is superior.

Jedi Teaching 40:

The Universe follows the Ways of The Force in the same way a bow is drawn. The high position is lowered and the low position is raised. In this way, excess is reduced and balance is achieved.

Society's way is to force those who do not have enough to give to those who already have in excess.

Who in the world has so much that they afford to supplement the rest of the world?

Those who follow the Ways of The Force.

This is possible because those who follow the Ways of The Force perform works and expect nothing in kind. They earn merits and accolades but claim no credit.

They bring no attention to their virtues.

Jedi Teaching 41:

In all the universe, nothing is as yielding and malleable as water. Yet nothing surpasses its ability to overcome the hard and strong. It has no equal in this quality.

Water demonstrates two of the aspects of The Force:

First, that which is flexible and yielding overcomes the strong and forceful.

Second, soft and supple overcomes the hard and rigid.

In all the universe this is understood, yet so very few are able to practice it.

This is why the Jedi say: One who accepts the nation's most shameful scandals is a lord of society. And, one who is able to accept the nation's natural disasters is a lord of the world.

True words seem like paradoxes.

Jedi Teaching 42:

Resentment almost always leads to greater resentment. No good ever comes from this.

Thus the Jedi is mindful of their debts but concerns themselves not with who owes him and does not demand payment from anyone.

There is virtue to be found in mindfulness of your debts. There is no virtue in being attentive of other's debts and people who are indebted to you.

The Force is unbiased. Followers of The Force seek this nature.

Jedi Teaching 43:

In the time of the Ancient Jedi Order, people lived in smaller communities. Cities were smaller and spread across the coastal areas of the world. People respected the ways of The Force and governed their passions. They respected death and did not travel far, and did not seek adventure and possessions.

Nomadic peoples wandered the lands and were not meddled with. All of the groups lived in unity with each other at peace and without want.

The Ancient Jedi had very sophisticated and advanced tools but did not rely on them. They had technological advances we can hardly fathom, but rarely used them. They had massive ships to sail the oceans with and transports to move from place to place but only used them on occasion.

They had the advanced weapons and armor but had no need for them.

Imagine if we could return to that time. A simpler time when people lived in accord with each other and the universe.

In their time, the food was simple but was sweet and fulfilling. The clothing they wore was plain yet there was beauty in it. The homes they lived in were secure and comfortable, and the customs they lived by were pleasing and enjoyable.

Neighbors and cities are close enough to see each other and to hear each other's dogs barking and children playing. Yet, the people lived out their lives, grew old and died without having ever been a burden to their each other.

Jedi Teaching 44:

Words which are true and have value, are often not pleasing to the ear. Words that are formed to be pleasing to the ear, often hold little truth.

Likewise, the truth need not argue and prove itself, and those who argue and push their points are not often truthful.

The wisest among us are not always the most educated, and those with the best educations are not always the wisest.

The Jedi meditate on letting go of things. They know that in doing so, self-fulfillment can be found, and that in the act of giving to others self-fulfillment can be multiplied.

The Way of The Force benefits all and harms none, even though this may not always be clear.

The Path of the Jedi is to find ways to accomplish things without striving.